T

Thoughts on the Education of Daughters, M. Wollstonecraft
Jazzybee Verlag Jürgen Beck
86450 Altenmünster, Loschberg 9
Deutschland

ISBN: 9783849681012

www.jazzybee-verlag.de
admin@jazzybee-verlag.de

Cover Design: Based on Mary Wollstonecraft -
http://europeana.eu/portal/record/2022611/H_DF_DF_1759.html. Marit
Kjeksrud Amundsen; Larvik Museum - avd av Vestfoldmuseene IKS. Larvik Museum
- avd av Vestfoldmuseene IKS - http://digitaltmuseum.no/011085442827. CC BY-
SA - http://creativecommons.org/licenses/by-sa/3.0/

Printed by Createspace, North Charleston, SC, USA

CONTENTS:

PREFACE.

IN the following pages I have endeavoured to point out some important things with respect to female education. It is true, many treatises have been already written; yet it occurred to me, that much still remained to be said. I shall not swell these sheets by writing apologies for my attempt. I am afraid, indeed, the reflections will, by some, be thought too grave; but I could not make them less so without writing affectedly; yet, though they may be insipid to the gay, others may not think them so; and if they should prove useful to one fellow-creature, and beguile any hours, which sorrow has made heavy, I shall think I have not been employed in vain.

THE NURSERY.

AS I conceive it to be the duty of every rational creature to attend to its offspring, I am sorry to observe, that reason and duty together have not so powerful an influence over human conduct, as instinct has in the brute creation. Indolence, and a thoughtless disregard of every thing, except the present indulgence, make many mothers, who may have momentary starts of tenderness, neglect their children. They follow a pleasing impulse, and never reflect that reason should cultivate and govern those instincts which are implanted in us to render the path of duty pleasant—for if they are not governed they will run wild; and strengthen the passions which are ever endeavouring to obtain dominion—I mean vanity and self-love.

The first thing to be attended to, is laying the foundation of a good constitution. The mother (if there are not very weighty reasons to prevent her) ought to suckle her children. Her milk is their proper nutriment, and for some time is quite sufficient. Were a regular mode of suckling adopted, it would be far from being a laborious talk. Children, who are left to the care of ignorant nurses, have their stomachs overloaded with improper food, which turns acid, and renders them very uncomfortable. We should be particularly careful to guard them in their infant state from bodily pain; as their minds can then afford them no amusement to alleviate it. The first years of a child's life are frequently made miserable through negligence or ignorance. Their complaints are mostly in their stomach or bowels; and these complaints generally arise from the quality and quantity of their food.

The suckling of a child also excites the warmed glow of tenderness—Its dependant, helpless state produces an affection, which may properly be termed maternal. I have even felt it, when I have seen a mother perform that office; and am of opinion, that maternal tenderness arises quite as much from habit as instinct. It is possible, I am convinced, to acquire the affection of a parent for an adopted child; it is necessary, therefore, for a mother to perform the office of one, in order to produce in herself a rational affection for her offspring.

Children very early contract the manners of those about them. It is easy to distinguish the child of a well-bred person, if it is not left entirely to the nurse's care. These women are of course ignorant, and to keep a child quiet for the moment, they humour all its little caprices. Very soon does it begin to be perverse, and eager to be gratified in every thing. The usual mode of acting is complying with the humours sometimes, and contradicting them at others—just according to the dictates of an uncorrected temper. This the infant finds out earlier than can be imagined, and it gives rise to an affection devoid of respect. Uniformity of conduct is the only feasible method of creating both. An inflexible adherence to any rule that has been laid down makes children comfortable, and saves the mother and nurse much trouble, as they will not often contest, if they have not once conquered. They will, I am sure, love and respect a person who treats them properly, if some one else does not indiscreetly indulge them. I once heard a judicious father say, "He would treat his child as he would his horse: first convince it he was its master and then its friend." But yet a rigid style of behaviour is by no means to be adopted; on the contrary, I wish to remark, that it is only in the years of childhood that the happiness of a human being depends entirely on others—and to embitter those years by needless restraint is cruel. To conciliate affection, affection must be shown, and little proofs of it ought always to be given—let them not appear weaknesses, and they will sink deep into the young mind, and call forth its most amiable propensities. The turbulent passions may be kept down till reason begins to dawn.

In the nursery too, they are taught to speak; and there they not only hear nonsense, but that nonsense retailed out in such silly, affected tones, as must disgust;—yet these are the tones which the child first imitates, and its innocent playful manner renders them tolerable, if not pleasing; but afterwards they are not easily got the better of—nay, many women always retain the pretty prattle of the nursery, and do not forget to lisp, when they have learnt to languish.

Children are taught revenge and lies in their very cradles. If they fall down, or strike their heads against any thing, to quiet them they are bid return the injury, and their little hands held out to do it. When they cry, or are troublesome, the cat or dog is chastised, or some bugbear called to take them away; which only terrifies them at first, for they soon find out that the nurse means nothing by these dreadful threatenings. Indeed, so well do they discover the fallacy, that I have seen little creatures, who could scarcely speak, play over the same tricks with their doll or the cat.

How, then, when the mind comes under discipline, can precepts of truth be inforced, when the first examples they have had would lead them to practise the contrary?

Moral Discipline.

It has been asserted, "That no being, merely human, could properly educate a child." I entirely coincide with this author; but though perfection cannot be attained, and unforeseen events will ever govern human conduct, yet still it is our duty to lay down some rule to regulate our actions by, and to adhere to it, as consistently as our infirmities will permit. To be able to follow Mr. Locke's system (and this may be said of almost all treatises on education) the parents must have subdued their own passions, which is not often the case in any considerable degree.

The marriage state is too often a state of discord; it does not always happen that both parents are rational; and the weakest have it in their power to do most mischief.

How then are the tender minds of children to be cultivated?— Mamma is only anxious that they should love her best, and perhaps takes pains to sow those seeds, which have produced such luxuriant weeds in her own mind. Or, what still more frequently occurs, the children are at first made play-things of, and when their tempers have been spoiled by indiscreet indulgence, they become troublesome, and are mostly left with servants; the first notions they imbibe, therefore, are mean and vulgar. They are taught cunning, the wisdom of that class of people, and a love of truth, the foundation of virtue, is soon obliterated from their minds. It is, in my opinion, a well-proved fact, that principles of truth are innate. Without reasoning we assent to many truths; we feel their force, and artful sophistry can only blunt those feelings which nature has implanted in us as instinctive guards to virtue. Dissimulation and cunning will soon drive all other good qualities before them, and deprive the mind of that beautiful simplicity, which can never be too much cherished.

Indeed it is of the utmost consequence to make a child artless, or to speak with more propriety, not to teach them to be otherwise; and in order to do so we must keep them out of the way of bad examples. Art is almost always practised by servants, and the same methods which children observe them to use, to shield themselves from blame, they will adopt—and cunning is so nearly allied to falsehood, that it will infallibly lead to it— it—or some foolish prevaricating subterfuge will occur, to silence any reproaches of the mind which may arise, if an attention to truth has been inculcated.

Another cause or source of art is injudicious correction. Accidents or giddy tricks are too frequently punished, and if children can conceal these, they will, to avoid chastisement. Restrain them, therefore, but never correct them without a very sufficient cause; such as a violation of truth, cruelty to animials, inferiors, or those kind of follies which lead to vice.

Children should be permitted to enter into conversation; but it requires great discernment to find out such subjects as will gradually improve them. Animals are the first objects which catch their attention; and I think little stories about them would not only amuse but instruct at the same time, and have the best effect in forming the temper and cultivating the good dispositions of the heart. There are many little books which have this tendency. One in particular I recollect: The Perambulations of a Mouse. I cannot here help mentioning a book of hymns, in measured prose written by the ingenious author of many other proper lessons for children. These hymns, I imagine, would contribute to fill the heart with religious sentiments and affections; and, if I may be allowed the expression, make the Deity obvious to the senses. The understanding, however, should not be overloaded any more than the stomach. Intellectual improvements, like the growth and formation of the body, must be gradual—yet there is no reason why the mind should lie fallow, while its "frail tenement" is imperceptibly fitting itself for a more reasonable inhabitant. It will not lie fallow; promiscuous seeds will be sown by accident, and they will shoot up with the wheat, and perhaps never be eradicated.

Whenever a child asks a question, it should always have a reasonable answer given it. Its little passions should be engaged. They are mostly fond of stories, and proper ones would improve them even while they are amused. Instead of these, their heads are filled with improbable tales, and superstitious accounts of invisible beings, which breed strange prejudices and vain fears in their minds.

The lisp of the nursery is confirmed, and vulgar phrases are acquired; which children, if possible, should never hear. To be able to express the thoughts with facility and propriety, is of great consequence in life, and if children were never led astray in this particular, it would prevent much trouble.

The riot too of the kitchen, or any other place where children are left only with servants, makes the decent restraint of the parlour irksome. A girl, who has vivacity, soon grows a romp; and if there are male servants, they go out a walking with them, and will frequently take little freedoms with Miss, the bearing with which gives a forwardness to her air, and makes her pert. The becoming modesty, which being accustomed to converse with superiors, will give a girl, is entirely done away. I must own, I am quite charmed when I see a sweet young creature, shrinking as it were from observation, and listening rather than talking. It is possible a girl may have this manner without having a very good understanding. If it should be so, this diffidence prevents her from being troublesome.

It is the duty of a parent to preserve a child from receiving wrong impressions.—As to prejudices, the first notions we have deserve that name; for it is not till we begin to waver in our opinions, that we exert our reason to examine them—and then, if they are received, they may be called our own.

The first things, then, that children ought to be encouraged to observe, are a strict adherence to truth; a proper submission to superiors; and condescension to inferiors. These are the main articles; but there are many others, which compared to them are trivial, and yet are of importance. It is not pleasing to see a child full of bows and grimaces; yet they need not be suffered to be rude. They should be employed, and such fables and tales may be culled out for them as would excite their curiosity. A taste for the beauties of nature should be very early cultivated: many things, with respect to the vegetable and animal world, may be explained in an amusing way; and this is an innocent source of pleasure within every one's reach.

5

Above all, try to teach them to combine their ideas. It is of more use than can be conceived, for a child to learn to compare things that are similar in some respects, and different in others. I wish them to be taught to think—thinking, indeed, is a severe exercise, and exercise of either mind or body will not at first be entered on, but with a view to pleasure. Not that I would have them make long reflections; for when they do not arise from experience, they are mostly absurd.

EXTERIOR ACCOMPLISHMENTS.

UNDER this head may be ranked all those accomplishments which merely render the person attractive; and those half-learnt ones which do not improve the mind. "A little learning of any kind is a dangerous thing;" and so far from making a person pleasing, it has the contrary effect.

Parents have mostly some weighty weighty business in hand, which they make a pretext to themselves for neglecting the arduous task of educating their children; they are therefore sent to school, and the allowance for them is so low, that the person who undertakes the charge must have more than she can possibly attend to; of course, the mechanical parts of education can only be observed. I have known children who could repeat things in the order they learnt them, that were quite at a loss when put out of the beaten track. If the understanding is not exercised, the memory will be employed to little purpose.

Girls learn something of music, drawing, and geography; but they do not know enough to engage their attention, and render it an employment of the mind. If they can play over a few tunes to their acquaintance, and have a drawing or two (half done by the master) to hang up in their rooms, they imagine themselves artists for the rest of their lives. It is not the being able to execute a trifling landscape, or any thing of the kind, that is of consequence—These are at best but trifles, and the foolish, indiscriminate praises which are bestowed on them only produce vanity. But what is really of no importance, when considered in this light, becomes of the utmost, when a girl has a fondness for the art, and a desire of excellence. Whatever tends to make a person in some measure independent of the senses, is a prop to virtue. Amusing employments must first occupy the mind; and as an attention to moral duties leads to piety, so whoever weighs one subject will turn to others, and new ideas will rush into the mind. The faculties will be exercised, and not suffered to sleep, which will give a variety to the character.

Dancing and elegance of manners are very pleasing, if too great a stress is not laid on them. These acquirements catch the senses, and open the way to the heart; but unsupported by solid good qualities, their reign is short.

The lively thoughtlessness of youth makes every young creature agreeable for the time; but when those years are flown, and sense is not substituted in the stead of vivacity, the follies of youth are acted over, and they never consider, that the things which please in their proper season, disgust out of it. It is very absurd to see a woman, whose brow time has marked with wrinkles, aping the manners of a girl in her teens.

I do not think it foreign to the present subject to mention the trifling conversations women are mostly fond of. In general, they are prone to ridicule. As they lay the greatest stress on manners, the most respectable characters will not escape its lash, if deficient in this article. Ridicule has been, with some people, the boasted test of truth—if so, our sex ought to make wonderful improvements; but I am apt to think, they often exert this talent till they lose all perception of it themselves. Affectation, and not ignorance, is the fair game for ridicule; and even affectation some good-natured persons will spare. We should never give pain without a design to amend.

Exterior accomplishments are not to be despised, if the acquiring of them does not satisfy the possessors, and prevent their cultivating the more important ones.

ARTIFICIAL MANNERS.

IT may be thought, that artificial manners and exterior accomplishments are much the same; but I think the former take a far wider range, and are materially different. The one arises from affectation, and the other seems only an error in judgment.

The emotions of the mind often appear conspicuous in the countenance and manner. These emotions, when they arise from sensibility and virtue, are inexpressibly pleasing. But it is easier to copy the cast of countenance, than to cultivate the virtues which animate and improve it.

How many people are like whitened sepulchres, and careful only about appearances! yet if we are too anxious to gain the approbation of the world, we must often forfeit our own.

How bewitching is that humble softness of manners which humility gives birth to, and how faint are the imitations of affectation! That gentleness of behaviour, which makes us courteous to all, and that benevolence, which makes us loth to offend any, and studious to please every creature, is sometimes copied by the polite; but how aukward is the copy! The warmest professions of regard are prostituted on all occasions. No distinctions are made, and the esteem which is only due to merit, appears to be lavished on all—Nay, affection is affected; at least, the language is borrowed, when there is no glow of it in the heart. Civility is due to all, but regard or admiration should never be expressed when it is not felt.

As humility gives the most pleasing cast to the countenance, so from sincerity arises that artlessnes of manners which is so engaging. She who suffers herself to be seen as she really is, can never be thought affected. She is not solicitous to act a part; her endeavour is not to hide; but correct her failings, and her face has of course that beauty, which an attention to the mind only gives. I never knew a person really ugly, who was not foolish or vicious; and I have seen the most beautiful features deformed by passion and vice. It is true, regular features strike at first; but it is a well ordered mind which occasions those turns of expression in the countenance, which make a lasting impression.

Feeling is ridiculous when affected; and even when felt, ought not to be displayed. It will appear if genuine; but when pushed forward to notice, it is obvious vanity has rivalled sorrow, and that the prettiness of the thing is thought of. Let the manners arise from the mind, and let there be no disguise for the genuine emotions of the heart.

Things merely ornamental are soon disregarded, and disregard can scarcely be borne when there is no internal support.

To have in this uncertain world some stay, which cannot be undermined, is of the utmost consequence; and this stay it is, which gives that dignity to the manners, which shews that a person does not depend on mere human applause for comfort and satisfaction.

DRESS.

MANY able pens have dwelt on the peculiar foibles of our sex. We have been equally desired to avoid the two extremes in dress, and the necessity of cleanliness has been insisted on, "As from the body's purity the mind receives a sympathetic aid."

By far too much of a girl's time is taken up in dress. This is an exterior accomplishment; but I chose to consider it by itself. The body hides the mind, and it is, in its turn, obscured by the drapery. I hate to see the frame of a picture so glaring, as to catch the eye and divide the attention. Dress ought to adorn the person, and not rival it. It may be simple, elegant, and becoming, without being expensive; and ridiculous fashions disregarded, while singularity is avoided. The beauty of dress (I shall raise astonishment by saying so) is its not being conspicuous one way or the other; when it neither distorts, or hides the human form by unnatural protuberances. If ornaments are much studied, a consciousness of being well dressed will appear in the face—and surely this mean pride does not give much sublimity to it.

"Out of the abundance of the heart the mouth speaketh." And how much conversation does dress furnish, which surely cannot be very improving or entertaining.

It gives rise to envy, and contests for trifling superiority, which do not render a woman very respectable to the other sex.

Arts are used to obtain money; and much is squandered away, which if saved for charitable purposes, might alleviate the distress of many poor families, and soften the heart of the girl who entered into such scenes of woe.

In the article of dress may be included the whole tribe of beauty-washes, cosmetics, Olympian dew, oriental herbs, liquid bloom, and the paint which enlivened Ninons face, and bid defiance to time. These numerous and essential articles are advertised in so ridiculous a style that the rapid sale of them is a very severe reflection on the understanding of those females who encourage it. The dew and herbs, I imagine, are very harmless, but I do not know whether the same may be said of the paint. White is certainly very prejudicial to the health, and never can be made to resemble nature. The red, too, takes off from the expression of the countenance, and the beautiful glow which modesty, affection, or any other emotion of the mind, gives, can never be seen. It is not "a mind-illumined face." "The body does not charm, because the mind is seen," but just the contrary; and if caught by it a man marries a woman thus disguised, he may chance not to be satisfied with her real person. A made-up face may strike visitors, but will certainly disgust domestic friends. And one obvious inference is drawn, truth is not expected to govern the inhabitant of so artificial a form. The false life with which rouge animates the eyes, is not of the most delicate kind; nor does a woman's dressing herself in a way to attract languishing glances, give us the most advantageous opinion of the purity of her mind.

I forgot to mention powder among the deceptions. It is a pity that it should be so generally worn. The most beautiful ornament of the features is disguised, and the shade it would give to the countenance entirely lost. The color of every person's hair generally suits the complexion, and is calculated to set it off. What absurdity then do they run into, who use red, blue, and yellow powder!—And what a false taste does it exhibit!

The quantity of pomatum is often disgusting. We laugh at the Hottentots, and in some things adopt their customs.

Simplicity of Dress, and unaffected manners, should go together. They demand respect, and will be admired by people of taste, even when love is out of the question.

THE FINE ARTS.

MUSIC and painting, and many other ingenious arts, are now brought to great perfection, and afford the most rational and delicate pleasure.

It is easy to find out if a young person has a taste for them. If they have, do not suffer it to lie dormant. Heaven kindly bestowed it, and a great blessing it is; but, like all other blessings, may be perverted: yet the intrinsic value is not lessened by the perversion. Should nature have been a niggard to them in this respect, persuade them to be silent, and not feign raptures they do not feel; for nothing can be more ridiculous.

In music I prefer expression to execution. The simple melody of some artless airs has often soothed my mind when it has been harrassed by care; and I have been raised from the very depths of sorrow, by the sublime harmony of some of Handel's compositions. I have been lifted above this little scene of grief and care, and mused on Him, from whom all bounty flows.

A person must have sense, taste, and sensibility, to render their music interesting. The nimble dance of the fingers may raise wonder, but not delight.

As to drawing, those cannot be really charmed by it, who do not observe the beauties of nature, and even admire them.

If a person is fond of tracing the effects of the passions, and marking the appearances they give to the countenance, they will be glad to see characters displayed on canvass, and enter into the spirit of them; but if by them the book of nature has not been read, their admiration is childish.

Works of fancy are very amusing, if a girl has a lively fancy; but if she makes others do the greatest part of them, and only wishes for the credit of doing them, do not encourage her.

Writing may be termed a fine art; and, I am sure, it is a very useful one. The style in particular deserves attention. Young people are very apt to substitute words for sentiments, and clothe mean thoughts in pompous diction. Industry and time are necessary to cure this, and will often do it. Children should be led into correspondences, and methods adopted to make them write down their sentiments, and they should be prevailed on to relate the stories they have read in their own words. Writing well is of great consequence in life as to our temporal interest and of still more to the mind; as it teaches a person to arrange their thoughts and digest them. Besides, it forms the only true basis of rational and elegant conversation.

Reading, and such arts as have been already mentioned, would fill up the time, and prevent a young person's being lost in dissipation, which enervates the mind, and often leads to improper connections. When habits are fixed, and a character in some measure formed, the entering into the busy world, so far from being dangerous, is useful. Knowledge will imperceptibly be acquired, and the taste improved, if admiration is not more sought for than improvement. For those seldom make observation who are full of themselves.

READING.

IT is an old, but a very true observation, that the human mind must ever be employed. A relish for reading, or any of the fine arts, should be cultivated very early in life; and those who reflect can tell, of what importance it is for the mind to have some resource in itself, and not to be entirely dependant on the senses for employment and amusement. If it unfortunately is so, it must submit to meanness, and often to vice, in order to gratify them. The wisest and best are too much under their influence; and the endeavouring to conquer them, when reason and virtue will not give their sanction, constitutes great part of the warfare of life. What support, then, have they who are all senses, and who are full of schemes, which terminate in temporal objects?

Reading is the most rational employment, if people seek food for the understanding, and do not read merely to remember words; or with a view to quote celebrated authors, and retail sentiments they do not understand or feel. Judicious books enlarge the mind and improve the heart, though some, by them, "are made coxcombs whom nature meant for fools."

Those productions which give a wrong account of the human passions, and the various accidents of life, ought not to be read before the judgment is formed, or at least exercised. Such accounts are one great cause of the affectation of young women. Sensibility is described and praised, and the effects of it represented in a way so different from nature, that those who imitate it must make themselves very ridiculous. A false taste is acquired, and sensible books appear dull and insipid after those superficial performances, which obtain their full end if they can keep the mind in a continual ferment. Gallantry is made the only interesting subject with the novelist; reading, therefore, will often co-operate to make his fair admirers insignificant.

I do not mean to recommend books of an abstracted or grave cast. There are in our language many, in which instruction and amusement are blended; the Adventurer is of this kind; I mention this book on account of its beautiful allegories and affecting tales, and similar ones may easily be selected, Reason strikes most forcibly when illustrated by the brilliancy of fancy. The sentiments which are scattered may be observed, and when they are relished, and the mind set to work, it may be allowed to chuse books for itself, for every thing will then instruct.

I would have every one try to form an opinion of an author themselves, though modesty may restrain them from mentioning it. Many are so anxious to have the reputation of taste, that they only praise the authors whose merit is indisputable. I am sick of hearing of the sublimity of Milton, the elegance and harmony of Pope, and the original, untaught genius of Shakespear. These cursory remarks are made by some who know nothing of nature, and could not enter into the spirit of those authors, or understand them.

A florid style mostly passes with the ignorant for fine writing; many sentences are admired that have no meaning in them, though they contain "words of thundering sound," and others that have nothing to recommend them but sweet and musical terminations.

Books of theology are not calculated for young persons; religion is best taught by example. The Bible should be read with particular respect, and they should not be taught reading by so sacred a book; lest they might consider that as a task, which ought to be a source of the most exalted satisfaction.

It may be observed, that I recommend the mind's being put into a proper train, and then left to itself. Fixed rules cannot be given, it must depend on the nature and strength of the understanding; and those who observe it can best tell what kind of cultivation will improve it. The mind is not, cannot be created by the teacher, though it may be cultivated, and its real powers found out.

The active spirits of youth may make time glide away without intellectual enjoyments; but when the novelty of the scene is worn off, the want of them will be felt, and nothing else can fill up the void. The mind is confined to the body, and must sink into sensuality; for it has nothing to do but to provide for it, "how it shall eat and drink, and wherewithal it shall be clothed."

All kinds of refinement have been found fault with for increasing our cares and sorrows; yet surely the contrary effect also arises from them. Taste and thought open many sources of pleasure, which do not depend on fortune.

No employment of the mind is at sufficient excuse for neglecting domestic duties, and I cannot conceive that they are incompatible. A woman may fit herself to be the companion and friend of a man of sense, and yet know how to take care of his family.

BOARDING-SCHOOLS.

If a mother has leisure and good sense, and more than one daughter, I think she could best educate them herself; but as many family reasons render it necessary sometimes to send them from home, boarding-schools are fixed on. I must own it is my opinion, that the manners are too much attended to in all schools; and in the nature of things it cannot be otherwise, as the reputation of the house depends upon it, and most people can judge of them. The temper is neglected, the same lessons are taught to all, and some get a smattering of things they have not capacity ever to understand; few things are learnt thoroughly, but many follies contracted, and an immoderate fondness for dress among the rest.

To prepare a woman to fulfil the important duties of a wife and mother, are certainly the objects that should be in view during the early period of life; yet accomplishments are most thought of, and they, and all-powerful beauty, generally gain the heart; and as the keeping of it is not considered of until it is lost, they are deemed of the most consequence. A sensible governess cannot attend to the minds of the number she is obliged to have. She may have been many years struggling to get established, and when fortune smiles, does not chuse to lose the opportunity of providing for old age; therefore continues to enlarge her school, with a view to accumulate a competency for that purpose. Domestic concerns cannot possibly be made a part of their employment, or proper conversations often entered on. Improper books will by stealth be introduced, and the bad example of one or two vicious children, in the play-hours, infect a number. Their gratitude and tenderness are not called forth in the way they might be by maternal affection. Many miseries does a girl of a mild disposition suffer, which a tender parent could guard her from. I shall not contest about the graces, but the virtues are best learnt at home, if a mother will give up her time and thoughts to the task; but if she cannot, they should be sent to school; for people who do not manage their children well, and have not large fortunes, must leave them often with servants, where they are in danger of still greater corruptions.

THE TEMPER.

THE forming of the temper ought to be the continual thought, and the first task of a parent or teacher. For to speak moderately, half the miseries of life arise from peevishness, or a tyrannical domineering temper. The tender, who are so by nature, or those whom religion has moulded with so heavenly a disposition, give way for the sake of peace—yet still this giving way undermines their domestic comfort, and stops the current of affection, they labor for patience, and labor is ever painful.

The governing of our temper is truly the business of our whole lives; but surely it would very much assist us if we were early put into the right road. As it is, when reason gains some strength, she has mountains of rubbish to remove, or perhaps exerts all her powers to justify the errors of folly and passion, rather than root them out.

A constant attention to the management of the temper produces gentleness and humility, and is practised on all occasions, as it is not done "to be seen of men." This meek spirit arises from good sense and resolution, and should not be confounded with indolence and timidity; weaknesses of mind, which often pass for good nature. She who submits, without conviction, to a parent or husband, will as unreasonably tyrannise over her servants; for slavish fear and tyranny go together. Resentment, indeed, may and will be felt occasionally by the best of human beings; yet humility will soon conquer it, and convert scorn and contempt into pity, and drive out that hasty pride which is always guarding Self from insult; which takes fire on the most trivial occasions, and which will not admit of a superior, or even an equal. With such a temper is often joined that bashful aukwardness which arises from ignorance, and is frequently termed diffidence; but which does not, in my opinion, deserve such a distinction. True humility is not innate, but like every other good quality must be cultivated. Reflections on miscarriages of conduct, and mistakes in opinion, sink it deep into the mind; especially if those miscarriages and mistakes have been a cause of pain—when we smart for our folly we remember it.

Few people look into their own hearts, or think of their tempers, though they severely censure others, on whose side they say the fault always lies. Now I am apt to believe, that there is not a temper in the world which does not need correction, and of course attention. Those who are termed good-humored, are frequently giddy, indolent, and insensible; yet because the society they mix with appear seldom displeased with a person who does not contest, and will laugh off an affront, they imagine themselves pleasing, when they are only not disagreeable. Warm tempers are too easily irritated. The one requires a spur, the other a rein. Health of mind, as well as body, must in general be obtained by patient submission to self-denial, and disagreeable operations.

If the presence of the Deity be inculcated and dwelt on till an habitual reverence is established in the mind, it will check the sallies of anger and sneers of peevishness, which corrode our peace, and render us wretched, without any claim to pity.

The wisdom of the Almighty has so ordered things, that one cause produces many effects. While we are looking into another's mind, and forming their temper, we are insensibly correcting our own; and every act of benevolence which we exert to our fellow-creatures, does ourselves the most essential services. Active virtue fits us for the society of more exalted beings. Our philanthrophy is a proof, we are told, that we are capable of loving our Creator. Indeed this divine love, or charity, appears to me the principal trait that remains of the illustrious image of the Deity, which was originally stampt on the soul, and which is to be renewed. Exalted views will raise the mind above trifling cares, and the many little weaknesses, which make us a torment to ourselves and others. Our temper will gradually improve, and vanity, which "the creature is made subject to," has not an entire dominion.

But I have digressed. A judicious parent can only manage a child in this important article; and example will best enforce precept.

Be careful, however, not to make hypocrites; smothered flames will blaze out with more violence for having been kept down. Expect not to do all yourself; experience must enable the child to assist you; you can only lay the foundation, or prevent bad propensities from settling into habits.

Unfortunate Situation of Females, fashionably educated, and left without a Fortune.

I Have hitherto only spoken of those females, who will have a provision made for them by their parents. But many who have been well, or at least fashionably educated, are left without a fortune, and if they are not entirely devoid of delicacy, they must frequently remain single.

Few are the modes of earning a subsistence, and those very humiliating. Perhaps to be an humble companion to some rich old cousin, or what is still worse, to live with strangers, who are so intolerably tyrannical, that none of their own relations can bear to live with them, though they should even expect a fortune in reversion. It is impossible to enumerate the many hours of anguish such a person must spend. Above the servants, yet considered by them as a spy, and ever reminded of her inferiority when in conversation with the superiors. If she cannot condescend to mean flattery, she has not a chance of being a favorite; and should any of the visitors take notice of her, and she for a moment forget her subordinate state, she is sure to be reminded of it.

Painfully sensible of unkindness, she is alive to every thing, and many sarcasms reach her, which were perhaps directed another way. She is alone, shut out from equality and confidence, and the concealed anxiety impairs her constitution; for she must wear a cheerful face, or be dismissed. The being dependant on the caprice of a fellow-creature, though certainly very necessary in this state of discipline, is yet a very bitter corrective, which we would fain shrink from.

A teacher at a school is only a kind of upper servant, who has more work than the menial ones.

A governess to young ladies is equally disagreeable. It is ten to one if they meet with a reasonable mother; and if she is not so, she will be continually finding fault to prove she is not ignorant, and be displeased if her pupils do not improve, but angry if the proper methods are taken to make them do so. The children treat them with disrespect, and often with insolence. In the mean time life glides away, and the spirits with it; "and when youth and genial years are flown," they have nothing to subsist on; or, perhaps, on some extraordinary occasion, some small allowance may be made for them, which is thought a great charity.

The few trades which are left, are now gradually falling into the hands of the men, and certainly they are not very respectable.

It is hard for a person who has a relish for polished society, to herd with the vulgar, or to condescend to mix with her former equals when she is considered in a different light. What unwelcome heart-breaking knowledge is then poured in on her! I mean a view of the selfishness and depravity of the world; for every other acquirement is a source of pleasure, though they may occasion temporary inconveniences. How cutting is the contempt she meets with!—A young mind looks round for love and friendship; but love and friendship fly from poverty: expect them not if you are poor! The mind must then sink into meanness, and accommodate itself to its new state, or dare to be unhappy. Yet I think no reflecting person would give up the experience and improvement they have gained, to have avoided the misfortunes; on the contrary they are thankfully ranked amongst the choicest blessings of life, when we are not under their immediate pressure.

How earnestly does a mind full of sensibility look for disinterested friendship, and long to meet with good unalloyed. When fortune smiles they hug the dear delusion; but dream not that it is one. The painted cloud disappears suddenly, the scene is changed, and what an aching void is left in the heart! a void which only religion can fill up — and how few seek this internal comfort!

A woman, who has beauty without sentiment, is in great danger of being seduced; and if she has any, cannot guard herself from painful mortifications. It is very disagreeable to keep up a continual reserve with men she has been formerly familiar with; yet if she places confidence, it is ten to one but she is deceived. Few men seriously think of marrying an inferior; and if they have honor enough not to take advantage of the artless tenderness of a woman who loves, and thinks not of the difference of rank, they do not undeceive her until she has anticipated happiness, which, contrasted with her dependant situation, appears delightful. The disappointment is severe; and the heart receives a wound which does not easily admit of a compleat cure, as the good that is missed is not valued according to its real worth: for fancy drew the picture, and grief delights to create food to feed on.

If what I have written should be read by parents, who are now going on in thoughtless extravagance, and anxious only that their daughters may be *genteelly educated*, let them consider to what sorrows they expose them; for I have not over-coloured the picture.

Though I warn parents to guard against leaving their daughters to encounter so much misery; yet if a young woman falls into it, she ought not to be discontented. Good must ultimately arise from every thing, to those who look beyond this infancy of their being; and here the comfort of a good conscience is our only stable support. The main business of our lives is to learn to be virtuous; and He who is training us up for immortal bliss, knows best what trials will contribute to make us so; and our resignation and improvement will render us respectable to ourselves, and to that Being, whose approbation is of more value than life itself. It is true, tribulation produces anguish, and we would fain avoid the bitter cup, though convinced its effects would be the most salutary. The Almighty is then the kind parent, who chastens and educates, and indulges us not when it would tend to our hurt. He is compassion itself, and never wounds but to heal, when the ends of correction are answered.

LOVE.

I Think there is not a subject that admits so little of reasoning on as love; nor can rules be laid down that will not appear to lean too much one way or the other. Circumstances must, in a great measure, govern the conduct in this particular; yet who can be a judge in their own case? Perhaps, before they begin to consider the matter, they see through the medium of passion, and its suggestions are often mistaken for those of reason. We can no other way account for the absurd matches we every day have an opportunity of observing; for in this respect, even the most sensible men and women err. A variety of causes will occasion an attachment; an endeavour to supplant another, or being by some accident confined to the society of one person. Many have found themselves entangled in an affair of honor, who only meant to fill up the heavy hours in an amusing way, or raise jealousy in some other bosom.

It is a difficult task to write on a subject when our own passions are likely to blind us. Hurried away by our feelings, we are apt to set those things down as general maxims, which only our partial experience gives rise to. Though it is not easy to say how a person should act under the immediate influence of passion, yet they certainly have no excuse who are actuated only by vanity, and deceive by an equivocal behaviour in order to gratify it. There are quite as many male coquets as female, and they are far more pernicious pests to society, as their sphere of action is larger, and they are less exposed to the censure of the world. A smothered sigh, downcast look, and the many other little arts which are played off, may give extreme pain to a sincere, artless woman, though she cannot resent, or complain of, the injury. This kind of trifling, I think, much more inexcusable than inconstancy; and why it is so, appears so obvious, I need not point it out.

People of sense and reflection are most apt to have violent and constant passions, and to be preyed on by them. Neither can they, for the sake of present pleasure, bear to act in such a manner, as that the retrospect should fill them with confusion and regret. Perhaps a delicate mind is not susceptible of a greater degree of misery, putting guilt out of the question, than what must arise from the consciousness of loving a person whom their reason does not approve. This, I am persuaded, has often been the case; and the passion must either be rooted out, or the continual allowances and excuses that are made will hurt the mind, and lessen the respect for virtue. Love, unsupported by esteem, must soon expire, or lead to depravity; as, on the contrary, when a worthy person is the object, it is the greatest incentive to improvement, and has the best effect on the manners and temper. We should always try to fix in our minds the rational grounds we have for loving a person, that we may be able to recollect them when we feel disgust or resentment; we should then habitually practise forbearance, and the many petty disputes which interrupt domestic peace would be avoided. A woman cannot reasonably be unhappy, if she is attached to a man of sense and goodness, though he may not be all she could wish.

I am very far from thinking love irresistible, and not to be conquered. "If weak women go astray," it is they, and not the stars, that are to be blamed. A resolute endeavour will almost always overcome difficulties. I knew a woman very early in life warmly attached to an agreeable man, yet she saw his faults; his principles were unfixed, and his prodigal turn would have obliged her to have restrained every benevolent emotion of her heart. She exerted her influence to improve him, but in vain did she for years try to do it. Convinced of the impossibility, she determined not to marry him, though she was forced to encounter poverty and its attendants.

It is too universal a maxim with novelists, that love is felt but once; though it appears to me, that the heart which is capable of receiving an impression at all, and can distinguish, will turn to a new object when the first is found unworthy. I am convinced it is practicable, when a respect for goodness has the first place in the mind, and notions of perfection are not affixed to constancy. Many ladies are delicately miserable, and imagine that they are lamenting the loss of a lover, when they are full of self-applause, and reflections on their own superior refinement. Painful feelings are prolonged beyond their natural course, to gratify our desire of appearing heroines, and we deceive ourselves as well as others. When any sudden stroke of fate deprives us of those we love, we may not readily get the better of the blow; but when we find we have been led astray by our passions, and that it was our own imaginations which gave the high colouring to the picture, we may be certain time will drive it out of our minds. For we cannot often think of our folly without being displeased with ourselves, and such reflexions are quickly banished. Habit and duty will co-operate, and religion may overcome what reason has in vain combated with; but refinement and romance are often confounded, and sensibility, which occasions this kind of inconstancy, is supposed to have the contrary effect.

Nothing can more tend to destroy peace of mind, than platonic attachments. They are begun in false refinement, and frequently end in sorrow, if not in guilt. The two extremes often meet, and virtue carried to excess will sometimes lead to the opposite vice. Not that I mean to insinuate that there is no such thing as friendship between persons of different sexes; I am convinced of the contrary. I only mean to observe, that if a woman's heart is disengaged, she should not give way to a pleasing delusion, and imagine she will be satisfied with the friendship of a man she admires, and prefers to the rest of the world. The heart is very treacherous, and if we do not guard its first emotions, we shall not afterwards be able to prevent its sighing for impossibilities. If there are any insuperable bars to an union in the common way, try to dismiss the dangerous tenderness, or it will undermine your comfort, and betray you into many errors. To attempt to raise ourselves above human beings is ridiculous; we cannot extirpate our passions, nor is it necessary that we should, though it may be wise sometimes not to stray too near a precipice, lest we fall over before we are aware. We cannot avoid much vexation and sorrow, if we are ever so prudent; it is then the part of wisdom to enjoy those gleams of sunshine which do not endanger our innocence, or lead to repentance. Love gilds all the prospects of life, and though it cannot always exclude apathy, it makes many cares appear trifling. Dean Swift hated the world, and only loved particular persons; yet pride rivalled them. A foolish wish of rising superior to the common wants and desires of the human species made him singular, but not respectable. He sacrificed an amiable woman to his caprice, and made those shun his company who would have been entertained and improved by his conversation, had he loved any one as well as himself. Universal benevolence is the first duty, and we should be careful not to let any passion so engross our thoughts, as to prevent our practising it. After all the dreams of rapture, earthly pleasures will not fill the mind, or support it when they have not the sanction of reason, or are too much depended on. The tumult of passion will subside, and even the pangs of disappointment cease to be felt. But for the wicked there is a worm that never dies—a guilty conscience. While that calm satisfaction which resignation produces, which cannot be described, but may be attained, in some degree, by those who try to keep in the strait, though thorny path which leads to bliss, shall sanctify the sorrows, and dignify the character of virtue.

MATRIMONY.

Early marriages are, in my opinion, a stop to improvement. If we were born only "to draw nutrition, propagate and rot," the sooner the end of creation was answered the better; but as women are here allowed to have souls, the soul ought to be attended to. In youth a woman endeavours to please the other sex, in order, generally speaking, to get married, and this endeavour calls forth all her powers. If she has had a tolerable education, the foundation only is laid, for the mind does not soon arrive at maturity, and should not be engrossed by domestic cares before any habits are fixed. The passions also have too much influence over the judgment to suffer it to direct her in this most important affair; and many women, I am persuaded, marry a man before they are twenty, whom they would have rejected some years after. Very frequently, when the education has been neglected, the mind improves itself, if it has leisure for reflection, and experience to reflect on; but how can this happen when they are forced to act before they have had time to think, or find that they are unhappily married? Nay, should they be so fortunate as to get a good husband, they will not set a proper value on him; he will be found much inferior to the lovers described in novels, and their want of knowledge makes them frequently disgusted with the man, when the fault is in human nature.

When a woman's mind has gained some strength, she will in all probability pay more attention to her actions than a girl can be expected to do; and if she thinks seriously, she will chuse for a companion a man of principle; and this perhaps young people do not sufficiently attend to, or see the necessity of doing. A woman of feeling must be very much hurt if she is obliged to keep her children out of their father's company, that their morals may not be injured by his conversation; and besides, the whole arduous task of education devolves on her, and in such a case it is not very practicable. Attention to the education of children must be irksome, when life appears to have so many charms, and its pleasures are not found fallacious. Many are but just returned from a boarding-school, when they are placed at the bead of a family, and how fit they are to manage it, I leave the judicious to judge. Can they improve a child's understanding, when they are scarcely out of the state of childhood themselves?

Dignity of manners, too, and proper reserve are often wanting. The constant attendant on too much familiarity is contempt. Women are often before marriage prudish, and afterwards they think they may innocently give way to fondness, and overwhelm the poor man with it. They think they have a legal right to his affections, and grow remiss in their endeavours to please. There are a thousand nameless decencies which good sense gives rise to, and artless proofs of regard which flow from the heart, and will reach it, if it is not depraved. It has ever occurred to me, that is was sufficient for a woman to receive caresses, and not bestow them. She ought to distinguish between fondness and tenderness. The latter is the sweetest cordial of life; but, like all other cordials, should be reserved for particular occasions; to exhilarate the spirits, when depressed by sickness, or lost in sorrow. Sensibility will best instruct. Some delicacies can never be pointed out or described, though they sink deep into the heart, and render the hours of distress supportable.

A woman should have so proper a pride, as not easily to forget a deliberate affront; though she must not too hastily resent any little coolness. We cannot always feel alike, and all are subject to changes of temper without an adequate cause.

Reason must often be called in to fill up the vacuums of life; but too many of our sex suffer theirs to lie dormant. A little ridicule and smart turn of expression, often confutes without convincing; and tricks are played off to raise tenderness, even while they are forfeiting esteem.

Women are said to be the weaker vessel, and many are the miseries which this weakness brings on them. Men have in some respects very much the advantage. If they have a tolerable understanding, it has a chance to be cultivated. They are forced to see human nature as it is, and are not left to dwell on the pictures of their own imaginations. Nothing, I am sure, calls forth the faculties so much as the being obliged to struggle with the world; and this is not a woman's province in a married state. Her sphere of action is not large, and if she is not taught to look into her own heart, how trivial are her occupations and pursuits! What little arts engross and narrow her mind! "Cunning fills up the mighty void of sense," and cares, which do not improve the heart or understanding, take up her attention. Of course, she falls a prey to childish anger, and silly capricious humors, which render her rather insignificant than vicious.

In a comfortable situation, a cultivated mind is necessary to render a woman contented; and in a miserable one, it is her only consolation. A sensible, delicate woman, who by some strange accident, or mistake, is joined to a fool or a brute, must be wretched beyond all names of wretchedness, if her views are confined to the present scene. Of what importance, then, is intellectual improvement, when our comfort here, and happiness hereafter, depends upon it.

Principles of religion should be fixed, and the mind not left to fluctuate in the time of distress, when it can receive succour from no other quarter. The conviction that every thing is working for our good will scarcely produce resignation, when we are deprived of our dearest hopes. How they can be satisfied, who have not this conviction, I cannot conceive; I rather think they will turn to some worldly support, and fall into folly, if not vice. For a little refinement only leads a woman into the wilds of romance, if she is not religious; nay, more, there is no true sentiment without it, nor perhaps any other effectual check to the passions.

DESULTORY THOUGHTS.

As every kind of domestic concern and family business is properly a woman's province, to enable her to discharge her duty she should study the different branches of it. Nothing is more useful in a family than a little knowledge of physic, sufficient to make the mistress of it a judicious nurse. Many a person, who has had a sensible physician to attend them, have been lost for want of the other; for tenderness, without judgment, sometimes does more harm than good.

The ignorant imagine there is something very mysterious in the practice of physic. They expect a medicine to work like a charm, and know nothing of the progress and crisis of disorders. The keeping of the patient low appears cruel, all kind of regimen is disregarded, and though the fever rages, they cannot be persuaded not to give them inflammatory food, "How (say they) can a person get well without nourishment?"

The mind, too, should be soothed at the same time; and indeed, whenever it sinks, soothing is, at first, better than reasoning. The slackened nerves are not to be braced by words. When a mind is worried by care, or oppressed by sorrow, it cannot in a moment grow tranquil, and attend to the voice of reason.

St. Paul says, "No chastening for the present seemeth to be joyous; but grievous: nevertheless, afterwards it yieldeth the peaceable fruits of righteousness unto them which are exercised thereby." It is plain, from these words of the Apostle, and from many other parts of Scripture, that afflictions are necessary to teach us true wisdom, and that in spite of this conviction, men would fain avoid the bitter draught, though certain that the drinking of it would be conducive to the purifying of their hearts. He who made us must know what will tend to our ultimate good; yet still all this is grievous, and the heart will throb with anguish when deprived of what it loves, and the tongue can scarcely faulter out an acquiescence to the Divine Will, when it is so contrary to our own. Due allowance ought then to be made for human infirmities, and the unhappy should be considered as objects of compassion, rather than blame. But in a very different stile does consolatory advice generally run; for instead of pouring oil or wine into the wound, it tends to convince the unfortunate persons that they are weak as well as unhappy. I am apt to imagine, that sorrow and resignation are not incompatible; and that though religion cannot make some disappointments pleasant, it prevents our repining, even while we smart under them. Did our feelings and reason always coincide, our passage through this world could not justly be termed a warfare, and faith would no longer be a virtue. It is our preferring the things that are not seen, to those which are, that proves us to be the heirs of promise.

On the sacred word of the Most High, we rely with firm assurance, that the sufferings of the present life will work out a far more exceeding and eternal weight of glory; yet still they are allowed to be afflictions, which, though temporary, must still be grievous.

The difference between those who sorrow without hope, and those who look up to Heaven, is not that the one feel more than the other, for they may be both equally depressed; but the latter think of the peaceable fruits which are to result from the discipline, and therefore patiently submit.

I have almost run into a sermon,—and I shall not make an apology for it. Whatever contributes to make us compassionate and resolute, is of the utmost consequence; both these qualities are necessary, if we are confined to a sick chamber. Various are the misfortunes of life, and it may be the lot of most of us to see death in all its terrors, when it attacks a friend; yet even then we must exert our friendship, and try to chear the departing spirit.

THE BENEFITS WHICH
ARISE FROM DISAPPOINMENTS.

Most women, and men too, have no character at all. Just opinions and virtuous passions appear by starts, and while we are giving way to the love and admiration which those qualities raise, they are quite different creatures. It is reflection which forms habits, and fixes principles indelibly on the heart; without it, the mind is like a wreck drifted about by every squall. The passion that we think most of will soon rival all the rest; it is then in our power, this way, to strengthen our good dispositions, and in some measure to establish a character, which will not depend on every accidental impulse. To be convinced of truths, and yet not to feel or act up to them, is a common thing. Present pleasure drives all before it, and adversity is mercifully sent to force us to think.

In the school of adversity we learn knowledge as well as virtue; yet we lament our hard fate, dwell on our disappointments, and never consider that our own wayward minds, and inconsistent hearts, require these needful correctives. Medicines are not sent to persons in health.

It is a well-known remark, that our very wishes give us not our wish. I have often thought it might be set down as a maxim, that the greatest disappointment we can meet with is the gratification of our fondest wishes. But truth is sometimes not pleasant; we turn from it, and doat on an illusion; and if we were not in a probationary state, we should do well to thicken the cloud, rather than dispel it.

There are some who delight in observing moral beauty, and their souls sicken when forced to view crimes and follies which could never hurt them. How numerous are the sorrows which reach such bosoms! They may truly be called *human creatures*; on every side they touch their fellow-mortals, and vibrate to the touch. Common humanity points out the important duties of our station; but sensibility (a kind of instinct, strengthened by reflection) can only teach the numberless minute things which give pain or pleasure.

A benevolent mind often suffers more than the object it commiserates, and will bear an inconvenience itself to shelter another from it. It makes allowance for failings though it longs to meet perfection, which it seems formed to adore. The Author of all good continually calls himself, a God long-suffering; and those most resemble him who practise forbearance. Love and compassion are the most delightful feelings of the soul, and to exert them to all that breathe is the wish of the benevolent heart. To struggle with ingratitude and selfishness is grating beyond expression: and the sense we have of our weakness, though useful, is not pleasant. Thus it is with, us, when we look for happiness, we meet with vexations: and if, now and then, we give way to tenderness, of any of the amiable passions, and taste pleasure, the mind, strained beyond its usual tone, falls into apathy. And yet we were made to be happy! But our passions will not contribute much to our bliss, till they are under the dominion of reason, and till that reason is enlightened and improved. Then sighing will cease, and all tears will be wiped away by that Being, in whose presence there is fulness of joy.

A person of tenderness must ever have particular attachments, and ever be disappointed; yet still they must be attached, in spite of human frailty; for if the mind is not kept in motion by either hope or fear, it sinks into the dreadful state before-mentioned.

I have very often heard it made a subject of ridicule, that when a person is disappointed in this world, they turn to the next. Nothing can be more natural than the transition; and it seems to me the scheme of Providence, that our finding things unsatisfactory here, should force us to think of the better country to which we are going.

ON THE TREATMENT OF SERVANTS.

The management of servants is a great part of the employment of a woman's life; and her own temper depends very much on her behaviour to them.

Servants are, in general, ignorant and cunning; we must consider their characters, if we would treat them properly, and continually practise forbearance. The same methods we use with children may be adopted with regard to them. Act uniformly, and never find fault without a just cause; and when there is, be positive, but not angry. A mind that is not too much engrossed by trifles, will not be discomposed by every little domestic disaster; and a thinking person can very readily make allowance for those faults which arise from want of reflection and education. I have seen the peace of a whole family disturbed by some trivial, cross accident, and hours spent in useless upbraidings about some mistake which would never have been thought of, but for the consequences that arose from it. An error in judgment or an accident should not be severely reprehended. It is a proof of wisdom to profit by experience, and not lament irremediable evils.

A benevolent person must ever wish to see those around them confortable, and try to be the cause of that comfort. The wide difference which education makes, I should suppose, would prevent familiarity in the way of equality; yet kindness must be shewn, if we are desirous that our domestics should be attached to our interest and persons. How pleasing it is to be attended with a smile of willingness, to be consulted when they are at a loss, and looked up to as a friend and benefactor when they are in distress. It is true we may often meet with ingratitude, but it ought not to discourage us; the refreshing showers of heaven fertilize the fields of the unworthy, as well as the just. We should nurse them in illness, and our superior judgment in those matters would often alleviate their pains.

Above all, we owe them a good example. The ceremonials of religion, on their account, should be attended to; as they always reverence them to a superstitious degree, or else neglect them. We should not shock the faith of the meanest fellow-creature; nay more, we should comply with their prejudices; for their religious notions are so over-run with them, that they are not easily separated; and by trying to pluck up the tares, we may root up the wheat with them.

The woman who gives way to caprice and ill-humour in the kitchen, cannot easily smooth her brow when her husband returns to his fire-side; nay, he may not only see the wrinkles of anger, but hear the disputes at second-hand. I heard a Gentleman say, it would break any man's heart to hear his wife argue such a case. Men who are employed about things of consequence, think these affairs more insignificant than they really are; for the warmth with which we engage in any business increases its importance, and our not entering into them has the contrary effect.

The behaviour of girls to servants is generally in extremes; too familiar or haughty. Indeed the one often produces the other, as a check, when the freedoms are troublesome.

We cannot make our servants wise or good, but we may teach them to be decent and orderly, and order leads to some degree of morality.

THE OBSERVANCE OF SUNDAY.

The institution of keeping the seventh day holy was wisely ordered by Providence for two purposes. To rest the body, and call off the mind from the too eager pursuit of the shadows of this life, which, I am afraid, often obscure the prospect of futurity, and fix our thoughts on earth. A respect for this ordinance is, I am persuaded, of the utmost consequence to national religion. The vulgar have such a notion of it, that with them, going to church, and being religious, are almost synonymous terms. They are so lost in their senses, that if this day did not continually remind them, they would soon forget that there was a God in the world. Some forms are necessary to support vital religion, and without them it would soon languish, and at last expire.

It is unfortunate, that this day is either kept with puritanical exactness, which renders it very irksome, or lost in dissipation and thoughtlessness. Either way is very prejudicial to the minds of children and servants, who ought not to be let run wild, not confined too strictly; and, above all, should not see their parents or masters indulge themselves in things which are generally thought wrong. I am fully persuaded, that servants have such a notion of card-playing, that where-ever it is practised of a Sunday their minds are hurt; and the barrier between good and evil in some measure broken down. Servants, who are accustomed to bodily labour, will fall into as laborious pleasures, if they are not gently restrained, and some substitute found out for them.

Such a close attention to a family may appear to many very disagreeable; but the path of duty will be found pleasant after some time; and the passions being employed this way, will, by degrees, come under the subjection of reason. I mean not to be rigid, the obstructions which arise in the way of our duty, do not strike a speculatist; I know, too, that in the moment of action, even a well-disposed mind is often carried away by the present impulse, and that it requires some experience to be able to distinguish the dictates of reason from those of passion. The truth is seldom found out until the tumult is over; we then wake as from a dream, and when we survey what we have done, and feel the folly of it, we might call on reason and say, why sleepest thou? Yet though people are led astray by their passions, and even relapse after the most bitter repentance, they should not despair, but still try to regain the right road, and cultivate such habits as may assist them.

I never knew much social virtue to reside in a house where the sabbath was grossly violated.

ON THE MISFORTUNE OF FLUCTUATING PRINCIPLES.

If we look for any comfort in friendship or society, we must associate with those who have fixed principles with respect to religion; for without them, repeated experience convinces me, the most shining qualities are unstable, and not to be depended on.

It has often been a matter of surprise to me, that so few people examine the tenets of the religion they profess, or are christians through conviction. They have no anchor to rest on, nor any fixed chart to direct them in the doubtful voyage of life; how then can they hope to find the "haven of rest?" But they think not of it, and cannot be expected to forego present advantages. Noble actions must arise from noble thoughts and views; when they are confined to this world, they must be groveling.

Faith, with respect to the promise of eternal happiness, can only enable us to combat with our passions, with a chance of victory. There are many who pay no attention to revelation, and more, perhaps, who have not any fixed belief in it. The sure word of comfort is neglected; and how people can live without it, I can scarcely conceive. For as the sun renews the face of nature, and chases away darkness from the world, so does this, still greater blessing, have the same effect on the mind, and enlightens and cheers when every thing else fails.

A true sense of our infirmities is the way to make us christians in the most extensive sense of the word. A mind depressed with a weight of weaknesses can only find comfort in the promises of the Gospel. The assistance there offered must raise the humble soul; and the account of the atonement that has been made, gives a rational ground for resting in hope until the toil of virtue is over, and faith has nothing to be exercised on.

It is the fashion now for young men to be deists. And many a one has improper books sent adrift in a sea of doubts—of which there is no end. This is not a land of certainty; there is no confining the wandering reason, and but one clue to prevent its being lost in endless researches. Reason is indeed the heaven-lighted lamp in man, and may safely be trusted when not entirely depended on; but when it pretends to discover what is beyond its ken, it certainly stretches the line too far, and runs into absurdity. Some speculations are idle and others hurtful, as they raise pride, and turn the thoughts to subjects that ought to be left unexplored. With love and awe we should think of the High and Lofty One, that inhabiteth eternity! and not presume to say how He must exist who created us. How unfortunate it is, that man must sink into a brute, and not employ his mind, or else, by thinking, grow so proud, as often to imagine himself a superior being! It is not the doubts of profound thinkers that I here allude to, but the crude notions which young men sport away when together, and sometimes in the company of young women, to make them wonder at their superior wisdom! There cannot be any thing more dangerous to a mind, not accustomed to think, than doubts delivered in a ridiculing way. They never go deep enough to solve them, of course they stick by them; and though they might not influence their conduct, if a fear of the world prevents their being guilty of vices, yet their thoughts are not restrained, and they should be observed diligently, "For out of them are the issues of life." A nice sense of right and wrong ought to be acquired, and then not only great vices will be avoided, but every little meanness; truth will reign in the inward parts, and mercy will attend her.

I have indeed so much compassion for those young females who are entering into the world without fixed principles, that I would fain persuade them to examine a little into the matter. For though in the season of gaiety they may not feel the want of them, in that of distress where will they fly for succour? Even with this support, life is a labor of patience—a conflict; and the utmost we can gain is a small portion of peace, a kind of watchful tranquillity, that is liable to continual interruptions.

> "Then keep each passion down, however dear;
> "Trust me, the tender are the most severe.
> "Guard, while 'tis thine, thy philosophic ease,
> "And ask no joy but that of virtuous peace;
> "That bids defiance to the storms of fate:
> "High bliss is only for a higher state."

Thomson.

BENEVOLENCE.

This first, and most amiable virtue, is often found in young persons that afterwards grow selfish; a knowledge of the arts of others, is an excuse to them for practising the same; and because they have been deceived once, or have found objects unworthy of their charity—if any one appeals to their feelings, the formidable word Imposture instantly banishes the compassionate emotions, and silences science. I do not mean to confine the exercise of benevolence to alms-giving, though it is a very material part of it. Faith, hope, and charity, ought to attend us in our passage through this world; but the two first leave us when we die, while the other is to be the constant inmate of our breast through all eternity. We ought not to suffer the heavenly spark to be quenched by selfishness; if we do, how can we expect it to revive, when the soul is disentangled from the body, and should be prepared for the realms of love? Forbearance and liberality of sentiment are the virtues of maturity. Children should be taught every thing in a positive way; and their own experience can only teach them afterwards to make distinctions and allowances. It is then the inferior part of benevolence that comes within their sphere of action, and it should not be suffered to sleep. Some part of the money that is allowed them for pocket-money, they should be encouraged to lay out this way, and the short-lived emotions of pity continually retraced 'till they grow into habits.

I knew a child that would, when very young, sit down and cry if it met a poor person, after it had laid out its money in cakes; this occurred once or twice, and the tears were shed with additional distress every time; till at last it resisted the temptation, and saved the money.

I think it a very good method for girls to have a certain allowance for cloaths. A mother can easily, without seeming to do it, observe how they spend it, and direct them accordingly. By these means they would learn the value of money, and be obliged to contrive. This would be a practical lesson of œconomy superior to all the theories that could be thought of. The having a fixed stipend, too, would enable them to be charitable, in the true sense of the word, as they would then give their own; and by denying themselves little ornaments, and doing their own work, they might increase the sum appropriated to charitable purposes.

A lively principle of this kind would also overcome indolence; for I have known people wasteful and penurious at the same time; but the wastefulness was to spare themselves trouble, and others only felt the effects of their penury, to make the balance even.

Women too often confine their love and charity to their own families. They fix not in their minds the precedency of moral obligations, or make their feelings give way to duty. Good-will to all the human race should dwell in our bosoms, nor should love to individuals induce us to violate this first of duties, or make us sacrifice the interest of any fellow-creature, to promote that of another, whom we happen to be more partial to. A parent, under distressed circumstances, should be supported, even though it should prevent our saving a fortune for a child; nay more, should they be both in distress at the same time, the prior obligation should be first discharged.

Under this head may be included the treatment of animals. Over them many children tyrannize with impunity; and find amusement in tormenting, or wantonly killing, any infect that comes in their way, though it does them no injury. I am persuaded, if they were told stories of them, and led to take an interest in their welfare and occupations, they would be tender to them; as it is, they think man the only thing of consequence in the creation. I once prevented a girl's killing ants, for sport, by adapting Mr. Addison's account of them to her understanding. Ever after she was careful not to tread on them, lest she should distress the whole community.

Stories of insects and animals are the first that should rouse the childish passions, and exercise humanity; and then they will rise to man, and from him to his Maker.

CARD-PLAYING.

Card-playing is now the constant amusement, I may say employment, of young and old, in genteel life. After all the fatigue of the toilet, blooming girls are set down to card-tables, and the most unpleasing passions called forth. Avarice does not wait for grey hairs and wrinkles, but marks a countenance where the loves and graces ought to revel. The hours that should be spent in improving the mind, or in innocent mirth, are thus thrown away; and if the stake is not considerable enough to rouse the passions, lost in insipidity, and a habit acquired which may lead to serious mischief. Not to talk of gaming, many people play for more than they can well afford to lose, and this sours their temper. Cards are the universal refuge to which the idle and the ignorant resort, to pass life away, and to keep their inactive souls awake, by the tumult of hope and fear.

> "Unknown to them, when sensual pleasures cloy,
> "To fill the languid pause with finer joy;
> "Unknown those powers that raise the soul to flame,
> "Catch every nerve, and vibrate through the frame."

And, of course, this is their favourite amusement. Silent, stupid attention appears necessary; and too frequently little arts are practised which debase the character, and at best give it a trifling turn. Certainly nothing can be more absurd than permitting girls to acquire a fondness for cards. In youth the imagination is lively, and novelty gives charms to every scene; pleasure almost obtrudes itself, and the pliable mind and warm affections are easily wrought on. They want not those resources, which even respectable and sensible persons sometimes find necessary, when they see life, as it is unsatisfactory, and cannot anticipate pleasures, which they know will fade when nearly viewed. Youth is the season of activity, and should not be lost in listlessness. Knowledge ought to be acquired, a laudable ambition encouraged; and even the errors of passion may produce useful experience, expand the faculties, and teach them to know their own hearts. The most shining abilities, and the most amiable dispositions of the mind, require culture, and a proper situation, not only to ripen and improve them, but to guard them against the perversions of vice, and the contagious influence of bad examples.

THE THEATRE.

The amusements which this place afford are generally supposed the most rational, and are really so to a cultivated mind; yet one that is not quite formed may learn affectation at the theatre. Many of our admired tragedies are too full of declamation, and a false display of the passions. A heroine is often made to grieve ten or twenty years, and yet the unabated sorrow has not given her cheeks a pallid hue; she still inspires the most violent passion in every beholder, and her own yields not to time. The prominent features of a passion are easily copied, while the more delicate touches are overlooked. That start of Cordelia's, when her father says, "I think that Lady is my daughter," has affected me beyond measure, when I could unmoved hear Calista describe the cave in which she would live "Until her tears had washed her guilt away."

The principal characters are too frequently made to rise above human nature, or sink below it; and this occasions many false conclusions. The chief use of dramatic performances should be to teach us to discriminate characters; but if we rest in separating the good from the bad, we are very superficial observers. May I venture a conjecture?—I cannot help thinking, that every human creature has some spark of goodness, which their long-suffering and benevolent Father gives them an opportunity of improving, though they may perversely smother it before they cease to breathe.

Death is treated in too slight a manner; and sought, when disappointments occur, with a degree of impatience, which proves that the main end of life has not been considered. That fearful punishment of sin, and convulsion of nature, is too often exposed to public view. Until very lately I never had the courage even to look at a person dying on the stage. The hour of death is not the time for the display of passions; nor do I think it natural it should: the mind is then dreadfully disturbed, and the trifling sorrows of this world not thought of. The deaths on the stage, in spite of the boasted sensibility of the age, seem to have much the same effect on a polite audience, as the execution of malefactors has on the mob that follow them to Tyburn.

The worst species of immorality is inculcated, and life (which is to determine the fate of eternity) thrown away when a kingdom or mistress is lost. Patience and submission to the will of Heaven, and those virtues which render us useful to society, are not brought forward to view; nor can they occasion those surprising turns of fortune which most delight vulgar minds. The almost imperceptible progress of the passions, which Shakespeare has so finely delineated, are not sufficiently observed, though the start of the actor is applauded. Few tragedies, I think, will please a person of discernment, and their sensibility is sure to be hurt.

Young persons, who are happily situated, do well to enter into fictitious distress; and if they have any judicious person to direct their judgment, it may be improved while their hearts are melted. Yet I would not have them confine their compassion to the distresses occasioned by love; and perhaps their feelings might more profitably be roused, if they were to see sometimes the complicated misery of sickness and poverty, and weep for the beggar instead of the king.

Comedy is not now so censurable as it was some years ago; and a chaste ear is not often shocked with indecencies. When follies are pointed, out, and vanity ridiculed, it may be very improving; and perhaps the stage is the only place where ridicule is useful.

What I have said is certainly only applicable to those who go to see the play, and not to shew themselves and waste time. The most insignificant amusement will afford instruction to thinking minds, and the most rational will be lost on a vacant one.

Remarks on the actors are frequently very tiresome. It is a fashionable topic, and a thread-bare one; it requires great abilities, and a knowledge of nature, to be a competent judge; and those who do not enter into the spirit of the author, are not qualified to converse with confidence on the subject.

PUBLIC PLACES.

Under this head I rank all those places, which are open to an indiscriminate resort of company. There seems at present such a rage for pleasure, that when adversity does not call home the thoughts, the whole day is mostly spent in preparations and plans, or in actual dissipation. Solitude appears insupportable, and domestic comfort stupid. And though the amusements may not always be relished, the mind is so enervated it cannot exert itself to find out any other substitute. An immoderate fondness for dress is acquired, and many fashionable females spend half the night in going from one place to another to display their sinery, repeat commonplace compliments, and raise envy in their acquaintance whom they endeavour to outshine. Women, who are engaged in those scenes, must spend more time in dress than they ought to do, and it will occupy their thoughts when they should be better employed.

In the fine Lady how few traits do we observe of those affections which dignify human nature! If she has any maternal tenderness, it is of a childish kind. We cannot be too careful not to verge on this character; though she lives many years she is still a child in understanding, and of so little use to society, that her death would scarcely be observed.

Dissipation leads to poverty, which cannot be patiently borne by those who have lived on the vain applause of others, on account of outward advantages; these were the things they imagined of most consequence, and of course they are tormented with false shame, when by a reverse of fortune they are deprived of them.

A young innocent girl, when she first enters into gay scenes, finds her spirits so raised by them, that she would often be lost in delight, if she was not checked by observing the behaviour of a class of females who attend those places. What a painful train of reflections do then arise in the mind, and convictions of the vice and folly of the world are prematurely forced on it. It is no longer a paradise, for innocence is not there; the taint of vice poisons every enjoyment, and affectation, though despised, is very contagious. If these reflections do not occur, languor follows the extraordinary exertions, and weak minds fall a prey to imaginary distress, to banish which they are obliged to take as a remedy what produced the disease.

We talk of amusements unbending the mind; so they ought; yet even in the hours of relaxation we are acquiring habits. A mind accustomed to observe can never be quite idle, and will catch improvement on all occasions. Our pursuits and pleasures should have the same tendency, and every thing concur to prepare us for a state of purity and happiness. There vice and folly will not poison our pleasures; our faculties will expand, and not mistake their object; and we shall no longer "see as through a glass darkly, but know, even as we are known."

Printed in Great Britain
by Amazon